written by QUINA ARAGON • illustrated by ADAM GRASON

HARVEST HOUSE PUBLISHERS
EUGENE, OREGON

To Jaelynn, BellaMia, Trey, Jael, Gianni, and Lauren.
Can you imagine all the love God has for you?
The best news is, we can't.

The quote of Romans 5:5 is from The ESV® Bible (The Holy Bible, English Standard Version®), copyright © 2001 by Crossway, a publishing ministry of Good News Publishers. Used by permission. All rights reserved.

Published in association with William K. Jensen Literary Agency, 119 Bampton Court, Eugene, Oregon 97404.
Cover design by Connie Gabbert Design and Illustration
Interior design by Left Coast Design

For bulk, special sales, or ministry purchases, please call 1 (800) 547-8979.
Email: Customerservice@hhpbooks.com

M is a federally registered trademark of the Hawkins Children's LLC. Harvest House Publishers, Inc., is the exclusive licensee of the trademark.

Love Can
Text copyright © 2023 by Quina Aragon
Artwork copyright © 2023 by Adam Grason
Published by Harvest House Publishers
Eugene, Oregon 97408
www.harvesthousepublishers.com

ISBN 978-0-7369-7440-0 (hardcover)
Library of Congress Control Number: 2022938675

Printed in China

22 23 24 25 26 27 28 29 30 / IM / 10 9 8 7 6 5 4 3 2 1

Before God made
the heavens and the earth,
He lived in perfect joy.

He delighted in Himself—
One forever-existing, perfect being,
Father, Son, and Spirit
—all One.

But God wasn't done . . .

The Father
made us with love,
but we turned away.

So He gave us His Son
so we could be saved.

Then before Jesus died and rose
and went back to heaven,

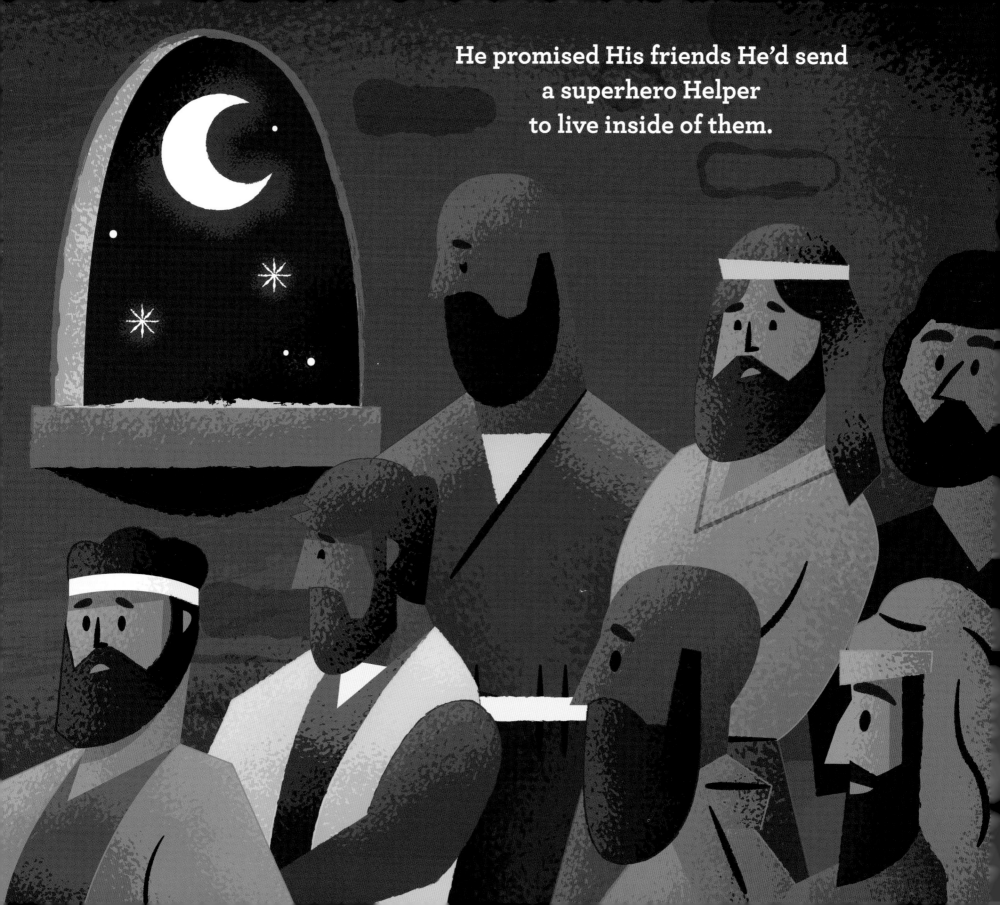

He promised His friends He'd send
a superhero Helper
to live inside of them.

The Holy Spirit is God,
just like the Father and the Son.

You can't see Him,
but He's not hiding from us.

Have you ever felt the wind
blow on your face?

Have you seen trees bend
in a hurricane?

You can't see the wind,
but you can see what it does.

And you can't see the Spirit,
but you can know He's around. How?

Now, if you're anything like me,
you sometimes dream
about having a superpower or two
(or three).

Like super strength
or super speed!

Or invisibility or jumping over buildings!
Flying! Mind reading! Time traveling!

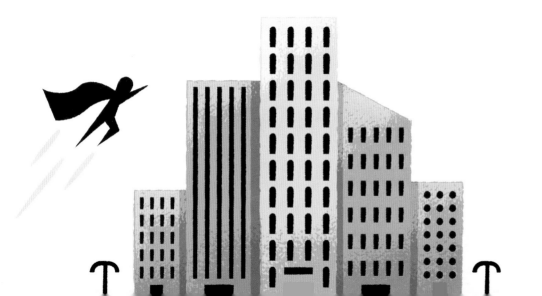

But what if you had
the superpower to love?

And I mean to love SO MUCH that your love made you look a lot like Jesus?

You see, the Spirit's got
a super-huge superhero job.

He's been doing it from the start.

The Holy Spirit connects us to God's loving heart.

Can you imagine the love
God has for His Son?

It's deeper than the ocean!
Wider than the sky!

It's higher than mountains!
But here's the surprise:

That same love God has for
His Son Jesus,

He has for every one of us
who believes in Him!

Don't you see? God is love—
the Father, the Spirit, the Son—
and Love loved so much,

Love came to live in us.

The Spirit helps us believe in Jesus
and tell others about Him too!

He gives us the superpower to show
all the things Love can do.

Love can be patient
when waiting in line.

Love can be kind
when no one is nice.

Love can share
even when it's hard.

Love can be honest
and not tell a lie.

But perhaps the
toughest thing
Love can do:
Love can forgive when
others hurt you.

So, what do you think?

Can you love like that
all by yourself?

Or do you think you might need
some superpower help?

I know I can't!
And neither can you.
But God is love,
and Love can. It's true!

That's why God gave us His Spirit.
So with Love in us . . .

LOVE TOO

GOD'S LOVE

HAS BEEN POURED INTO

OUR HEARTS

THROUGH THE

HOLY SPIRIT

WHO HAS BEEN

GIVEN TO US

ROMANS 5:5